HOW TO EFFECTIVELY MARKET AND PROMOTE FLASH SALES FOR YOUR BUSINESS?

Increase customer engagement and sales.

Rishi Pal Sharma

Super Flash Sales Chapters

1. **Define a goal.**
2. **Pick an In-Demand Offer**
3. **Choose a date.**
4. **Decide on Your Sale Offer**
5. **Determine how long it will run**
6. **Create marketing materials**
7. **Inform Existing Partners of the Upcoming Sale**
8. **Recruit and inform new marketing partners.**
9. **Take care of the technical aspects**
10. **Prepare customer service**
11. **Test and track sales copy**
12. **Prepare Your Own Emails and Blog Posts**
13. **Create a video**
14. **Prepare Facebook ads**
15. **Purchase Ads on High-Traffic Niche Sites**
16. **Start a Buzz on Social Media**
17. **Inform the payment processor**
18. **Set Up Backend Offers**
19. **Remind Partners of the Upcoming Sale**
20. **Send Out Emails To Your List**
21. **Email the Night Before**
22. **Upload the Offer Page**
23. **Test the entire sales process.**
24. **Send out Sale Day Materials**
25. **Publish Last Chance Materials**

Understanding how to effectively market and promote flash sales for your business is key to maximizing customer engagement and sales.

All about flash sales for your business understands how to effectively market and promote them to drive maximum customer engagement and sales.

Find out how to start and succeed in flash sales.

How to Turn a Few Days into a Financial Windfall!

The 25-Point Flash Sale Checklist for Creating Cash on Demand

A flash sale is a great way to generate a lot of sales and excitement in a very short period. The best way to do this is to plan it several weeks out, bring in your marketing partners to promote the event, and build anticipation among your prospects. The success of a flash sale is heavily dependent on effective marketing strategies and creating a sense of urgency among potential customers. One effective marketing strategy is to use social media platforms to create buzz and reach a wider audience. By utilizing eye-catching graphics, engaging captions, and limited-time offers, you can grab the attention of potential customers and encourage them to take immediate action. Additionally, offering exclusive discounts or bonuses for early bird purchasers can further enhance the sense of urgency and increase the likelihood of a financial windfall during your flash sale.

How do you do that? By following this 25-point checklist, take a look.

1. Define a goal.

The very first thing you need to do is define your goal for this sale. Ideally, you should have just one primary goal to focus on, though you may have secondary goals as well. These goals may include:

- *Customer acquisition. Increasing revenue. Building brand awareness. Clearing out excess inventory.*

- *Generate sales for front-end profits.* Determine your target audience. Whom are you trying to reach with this flash sale? Understanding your target audience will help you tailor your marketing efforts and messaging to effectively reach them.

Set a timeframe for your flash sale. Decide how long the sale will last, whether it is a few hours, a day, or a weekend. Creating a sense of urgency with a limited period can motivate customers to make a purchase sooner rather than later.

- *Boost backend profits.* Create a compelling offer or discount for your flash sale. Consider offering a significant discount, a buy-one-get-one deal, or a limited-time exclusive product to entice customers to take advantage of the sale.

Promote your flash sale through various marketing channels. Utilize social media, email marketing, and targeted advertisements to reach your target audience and create buzz around the sale.

Monitor and analyse the results of your flash sale. Track sales, customer feedback, and engagement metrics to evaluate the success of your promotion and identify areas for improvement in future sales events.

- *Create affiliate excitement.*

One way to create affiliate excitement is by offering special incentives or bonuses for affiliates who generate a certain number of sales during the flash sale. This can motivate affiliates to promote the sale more aggressively and increase their efforts to drive traffic and conversions. Additionally, consider hosting a contest or giveaway exclusively for affiliates, where they have the chance to win valuable prizes or exclusive access to future promotions. This can further incentivize affiliates to actively participate in promoting the flash sale and generate excitement among their audience.

- *Create a buzz in the niche about your products. One way to create a buzz in the niche about your products is by reaching out to influential bloggers or social media influencers in your industry and offering them exclusive discounts or early access to the flash sale. By doing so, you can leverage their large following and credibility to generate excitement and anticipation among their audience. Another strategy is to utilize email-marketing campaigns specifically targeting your affiliate network, providing them with pre-written promotional content and graphics that they can easily share with their own audience. This not only saves them time and effort but also ensures consistent messaging across different platforms, further amplifying the reach of your flash sale.*

- *Establish yourself as a "big player" in the niche. One way to establish yourself as a "big player" in the niche is by collaborating with influential bloggers or industry experts who can endorse your flash sale. Their endorsement can help build trust and credibility among your target audience, increasing the chances of them participating in the sale. Additionally, you can offer exclusive discounts or perks to loyal customers or members of your loyalty programme, making them feel valued and appreciated for their continued support. This can further solidify your position as a reputable and important player in the industry.*

- *Build your mailing lists. By consistently collecting email addresses from your customers and website visitors, you can build a strong mailing list. This allows you to directly communicate with your audience and inform them about upcoming flash sales, exclusive offers, and new product launches. Regularly sending out engaging and personalized emails can help keep your brand top of mind and encourage repeat purchases, further establishing your presence in the industry.*

- *Generate excitement about a particular product. One effective way to generate excitement about a particular product is by creating a buzz through social media platforms. Utilize captivating visuals, compelling captions, and interactive content to pique the interest of your target audience. Additionally, consider collaborating with influencers or conducting giveaways to create a sense of anticipation and exclusivity surrounding the product launch.*

Pick your primary goal, and then move onto the next step.

2. Pick an In-Demand Offer

No matter what your goal is, you need to promote an in-demand offer. Throwing a flash sale for one of your most popular products serves this purpose. However, you can also run a flash sale on a new offer—just make sure it's something your market really wants. By offering a limited-time discount or special bundle deal, you can create a sense of urgency and encourage immediate action from your audience. This will not only generate excitement but also drive sales and increase customer satisfaction. Additionally, conducting market research or surveys can help you

identify what your target audience desires, ensuring that the offer you promote aligns with their needs and preferences.

In other words, do your market research first! Specifically:

- *See what the hot sellers in your niche are in marketplaces like ClickBank.com, JVZoo.com, and even Amazon.com.*
- *Survey your market to see what they want.*
- *Take note of what the top marketers in your niche are selling on their websites, through their newsletters, and to their social media followers.*
- *Check out what type of products people are paying money to advertise on Google, on top sites in your niche, and even on Facebook.*
- *Use a keyword tool like WordTracker.com or MarketSamurai.com to uncover what your niche is looking for.*

Once you have a popular product, move on.

3. Choose a date.

Now choose a date for your flash sale. Keep these points in mind:

- *Choose a date that is at least two to three weeks away. This gives you and your affiliate's time to prepare.*
- *Research the date to find out if there is anything-major going on at the same time. For example, if a popular*

marketer in your niche is launching a huge product on the same date, you will have a harder time getting affiliates onboard and getting customers to take notice. Next...

4. Decide on Your Sale Offer

Here is where you decide on the following points:

· *What all will you include in the offer?*

For example, are you going to toss in an extra bonus or two to make the offer even more attractive?

· *What percentage off or discount are you offering? Hint: A flash sale should be an attractive offer, such as 40% off or more than the regular price.*

· *What percentage will you give to affiliates? This is partly going to depend on your goals. If you are looking at building a list, getting affiliates really involved, and generating backend profits, then you may consider giving all or most of the frontend commissions to affiliates. If you are looking at generating many frontend profits, then you can offer a more standard 50% commission rate for affiliates. (This is assuming you are selling digital products—commissions, of course, are smaller if you are selling physical products.)*

Next...

5. Determine how long it will run.

As the name implies, a flash sale happens fast; it is usually over in a matter of hours. Generally, this may be anywhere from four to twenty-four hours.

- *Determine the start and end times.*
- *Figure on running it for at least 8–12 hours for maximum exposure.*
- *Take your prospects' time zones and activities (such as work) into consideration when deciding the start and end times. In other words, you don't want the entire sale to fall*

within the work day; otherwise, you'll have a lot of people missing out.

Next...

6. Create marketing materials.

This is where you create sales materials for your marketing

partners for these three purposes:

- *To build anticipation for the sale in the week leading up to the sale day.*
- *To announce the sale itself.*
- *To send out one or more reminders about the sale during the actual sale day.*

Think about the communication channels both you and your affiliates use to reach prospects. Then create materials for these channels. For example:

- *Emails*
- *Blog posts*
- *Social media blurbs (short ones for Twitter, longer ones for platforms like Facebook).*
- *Text messages.*

Once you've created these materials, upload them to the affiliate centre for your partners' convenience.

Next...

7. Inform Existing Partners of the Upcoming Sale

If you already have a team of affiliates, then now is the time to inform them of the sale. Let them know the details of the sale, including the date, time, and any special promotions or discounts that will be offered. Encourage them to promote the sale to their audience, and provide them with any necessary materials or resources to make it easier for them to do so. Additionally, consider offering incentives or bonuses for affiliates who generate a certain amount of sales during the sale period. This will help motivate them to actively promote the sale and drive more traffic and sales to your business.

- *Tell them at least two weeks in advance of the sale so they have time to prepare. A longer lead time is preferable, as top affiliates usually have a full publishing schedule.*

- *Give your affiliates access to the product. This will allow them to familiarise themselves with the product and create more compelling content. Moreover, consider providing them with exclusive discount codes or special offers that* they can share with their audience, giving them an extra incentive to promote the sale.

- Let them know how to promote (e.g., how to obtain their affiliate link). Additionally, provide your affiliates with promotional materials such as banners, graphics, and sample social media posts. This will make it easier for them to promote the sale and ensure a consistent brand message across different platforms. Lastly, offer ongoing support and communication throughout the promotion period to address any questions or concerns they may have and to keep them engaged and motivated to promote your business.

- Tell them about the marketing materials inside the affiliate centre. These marketing materials can include email templates, product images, and videos that affiliates can use to effectively promote the sale. By providing these resources, affiliates will have a variety of options to choose from and can tailor their promotional efforts to their specific audience. This will ultimately increase their chances of success and drive more sales for your business.

- Generate excitement around the event—talk about the commissions they'll earn, the current conversion rate on the sales letter, etc.

- Give them a timeline so they know when to send out the pre-sale materials.

Next step...

8. Recruit and inform new marketing partners.

If you'd like to make a really big splash on sales day, then you may consider recruiting new affiliate partners. You can do this yourself, or you can hire an affiliate manager or JV broker to do it for you.

As always, it's easier to get people to say yes to your request if they already know, like, and trust you. Here's an example email or social media message you can send to these potential partners:

Subject line: I wanted you to be the first to know...

Hi [First Name],

[Your Name] is here from [your site]. I've got a flash sale coming up in [number of weeks], and I wanted to extend a personal invitation for you to join in on this unique event where you can generate [percent] commissions—that's [$ amount] for every sale you bring in.

Let me explain...

This sale is for the [name of product], which is a quick description of the product. This would be a good match for your audience because [explain reason].

You can take a look for yourself here: [download link]

This flash sale starts at [date and time] and ends [insert when it ends]. Because sales are so short, we're expecting conversion rates above and beyond the normal [percent conversion rates]. That means those [$ amount] commissions are going to add up fast!

I've already set everything up for you, so it's super easy for you to take part in this event.

Here's your affiliate link: [insert link]

Here's where you can get a complete set of emails and ads to promote the event: [insert link]

Shoot me an email back to let me know if you're on board! I look forward to working with you.

[sign off

p.s. Those who jump in early get the biggest commission rates. Hit reply to let me know you're in, and I'll boost your commission rate to [percentage].

9. Take care of the technical aspects.

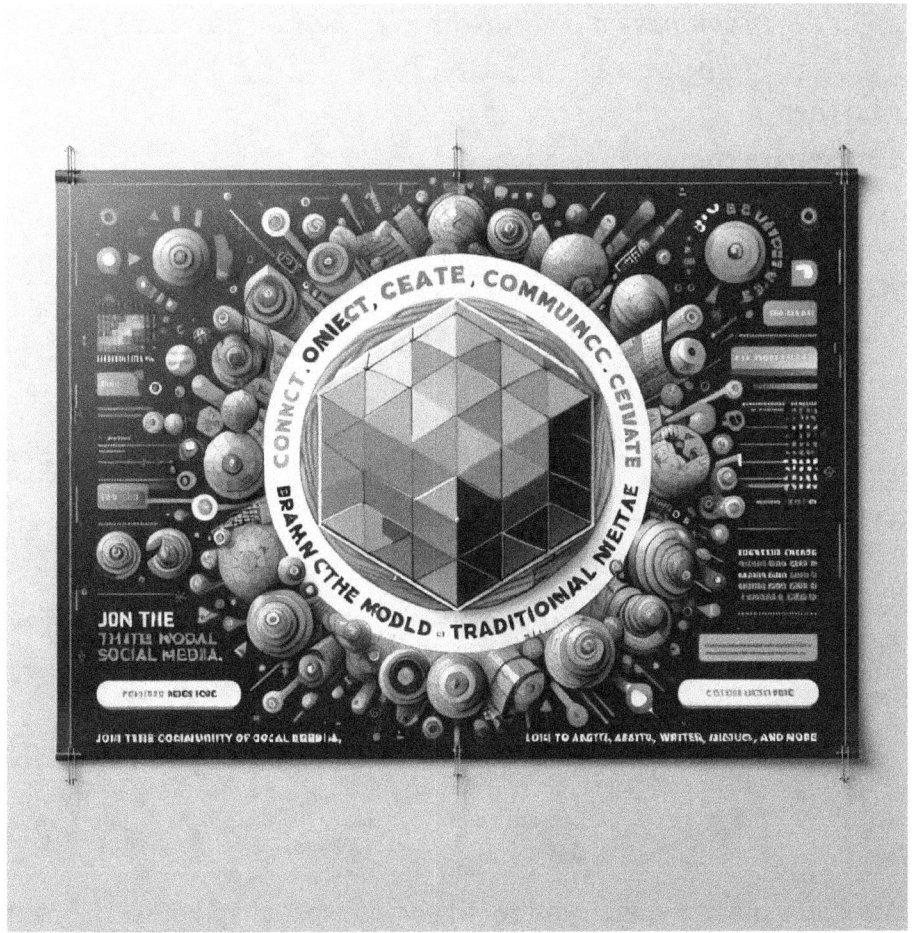

A popular, well-advertised flash sale can create a lot of traffic, and in turn, this heavy server load can create problems on your site. To ensure a smooth experience for your customers, make sure to optimise your website's server capacity and bandwidth. Consider consulting with a technical expert to handle any potential issues that may arise during the flash sale. That's why you'll want to do the following:

- *If you're not very technical, then hire a tech whiz to handle this step.*
- *Make sure your web hosting account can accommodate a big spike in traffic and requests.*

- *If you have a dedicated server, be sure it's ready for high traffic.*

And then...

10. Prepare customer service.

Another place where you're likely to see a spike is in your customer service requests. That's why you'll want to make sure your customer service is ready to handle the load. This includes:

- *Hiring additional help if needed.*
- *Training both new hires and existing staff on how to handle the inquiries that are likely to arise during the sale.*
- *Creating new FAQs and other materials to help cut down on customer service load during the sale.*
- *Offering multiple ways for prospects and customers to reach you, such as live chat and a help desk.*

And then...

11. Test and track sales copy.

The idea here is that you want to optimise your copy so that you get maximum conversions during the sale. 12. Implementing A/B testing to compare different versions of your sales copy and identify the most effective one. This will help you refine your messaging and increase the likelihood of converting prospects into customers.

13. Monitoring and analysing customer feedback during the sale to identify any pain points or areas for improvement in your sales copy. This feedback can be invaluable in making the necessary adjustments to optimise conversions and enhance the overall customer experience.

Steps to take:

- *Use a quick way to generate traffic for your testing, such as Google AdWords and Facebook ads.*

- *Focus on the factors that will have the most impact, such as the headline, bulleted benefit list, P.S., price, and call to action.*

Next step...

12. Prepare Your Own Emails and Blog Posts

You've already created materials for your affiliates and marketing partners. Now you need to create these same materials for yourself. This step is actually easy because, in most cases, all you have to do is tweak the affiliate materials.

For example, whereas an affiliate email may refer to "John Doe's new product," you would tweak this to first-person language such as "My new product."

13. Create a video.

The next step is to create a short sales video to help drum up excitement on the day of the flash sale. This is particularly important if your sales letter is a text letter, as offering a pre-sale video will help you reach more people. Creating a video is an effective way to engage potential customers and generate excitement for your flash sale. By showcasing the benefits and features of your product or service in a visually appealing format, you can capture the attention of a wider audience. Additionally, including a pre-sale video alongside your sales letter can help you connect with more people and increase the chances of conversions.

Pointers:

- *Keep it short—just two to three minutes long.*
- *Present a problem, highlight the signs of that problem, and then offer your product as the solution to the problem.*
- *Showcase the main benefits of your product.*
- *Provide a strong call to action, being sure to mention the flash sale to create urgency.*

On sale day, you'll be posting this on YouTube, on your social media pages, and on your blog.

The next step...

14. Prepare Facebook ads.

To generate extra excitement on sale day, you'll want to run some paid advertising. The Facebook ad platform is a good choice. The idea is to launch the ads on sale day, but of course you'll want to prepare them in advance. To prepare Facebook ads for your flash sale, create compelling visuals and persuasive copy that highlight the unique features and benefits of your product. Use eye-catching images or videos to grab the attention of your target audience and clearly communicate how your product can solve their problem. Don't forget to include a strong call to action in your ad, encouraging viewers to click through to your website and take advantage of the limited-time offer. Remember, time is of the essence, so make sure to schedule your ads to go live on sale day for maximum impact. This includes:

- *Choosing an eye-catching graphic.*
- *Writing your ad.*

- *Selecting the target audience using Facebook's ad platform editor.*
- *Setting it all up to start running at the appointed time and day.*
- *Double-check everything to be sure the links, start times, and end times are all correct.*

Next...

15. Purchase Ads on High-Traffic Niche Sites

Same as above—you'll want to prepare ads and set them to run on sale day. Most niche site owners set up and run ads manually, so you'll need to make arrangements with the owner and pay in advance. Next, you should monitor the performance of your ads and make any necessary adjustments to maximise their effectiveness. Once you have purchased ads on high-traffic niche sites, it is important to monitor their performance and make any necessary adjustments. Additionally, consider reaching out to influencers in your industry to promote your sale day and increase its impact even further.

16. Start a Buzz on Social Media

This includes:

- *Building anticipation for the upcoming sale.*
- *Sharing graphics, videos, or other content that is likely to go viral.*
- *Inserting a specific call to action and encouraging people to share the content.*

Next...

17. Inform the payment processor.

Your payment processor may suspect suspicious activity if

suddenly you have a huge sales surge without warning, and they could temporarily suspend your account. That's why you'll want to do two things:

- *Inform the payment processor of the expected surge. Ideally, you should speak to a human on the phone about this, get the representative's name, and ask them to email you about the call. (So you have proof that they were informed.)*

- *Make a "Plan B" in case your payment processor does go down. Just be sure that Plan B gives credit to affiliates, where applicable.*

Next step...

18. Set Up Backend Offers

If you haven't already done so, be sure to build out your sales funnel on the backend of this offer. This may include:

- *Inserting an order form upsells.*
- *Inserting backend offers in the product itself.*
- *Setting up an autoresponder sequence for these new customers with backend offers inserted into the sequence.*

Next...

19. Remind Partners of the Upcoming Sale

Your job is to remind all marketing partners of the approaching sale and let them know when to start promoting. So, for example:

- *Let them know two weeks before the sale that they can start promoting one week out.*
- *About a week and a half before the sale, let them know they can promote in three days.*
- *Remind them four days before the sale to do pre-selling.*
- *Remind them the night before the sale to promote it the next morning.*

· *Remind them on the day of the sale to promote hard.*

TIP: You can automate all of these emails by loading them into an auto responder.

Next...

20. Send Out Emails To Your List

Now you can start building anticipation by sending your pre-sale emails about one week before the sale starts and three or four days before the sale starts.

21. Email the Night Before

Now send out the final anticipation email the night before the sale to generate excitement. Be sure to list the benefits of the product as well as remind people of how short the sale period is.

22. Upload the Offer Page

Do this the morning of the sale.

23. Test the entire sales process.

Run through all the links, forms, and payment processor steps to make sure everything is in good working order.

24. Send out Sale Day Materials

When the sale starts, send out all the sales materials you previously created, including emails, blog posts, and social media posts.

25. Publish Last Chance Materials

Later in the day (a few hours before the sale ends), send out emails, blog posts, and social media posts reminding people that this is their last chance to get the product at an incredible discount.

Content writing....

Website Content

Copy Editing

Blog/Article Writing

Professional content and copy writing services for your business.

Conclusion

So there you have it—a complete 25-point checklist for running your very own super-profitable flash sale. Print this out and get to work setting up your sale today! Remember to monitor the performance of your flash sale throughout the day and make any necessary adjustments to maximise its success. Additionally, don't forget to analyse the results after the sale ends to gain insights for future sales strategies. Good luck with your flash sale!